Marike Fourie is a young author from South Africa who discovered her passion and talent for writing at the age of 22. She grew up loving mathematics and science, yet chose to drop out twice after attempting further studies in these fields. That's when her mission became self-discovery and self-actualization, to serve her purpose. She began by journaling and within a few months, the inspiration of the poetic trilogies arrived. She believes that she alone cannot take credit for her writing, since it comes from a force beyond that of the individual identity.

This book is dedicated to You;
may you take from it what you need.

Marike Fourie

MINE, YOURS, OURS

A 21st Century Poetic Trilogy

AUSTIN MACAULEY PUBLISHERS™
LONDON • CAMBRIDGE • NEW YORK • SHARJAH

Copyright © Marike Fourie 2022

The right of Marike Fourie to be identified as author of this work has been asserted by the author in accordance with Federal Law No. (7) of UAE, Year 2002, Concerning Copyrights and Neighboring Rights.

All rights reserved. No part of this publication may be reproduced, stored in a retrieval system, or transmitted in any form or by any means, electronic, mechanical, photocopying, recording, or otherwise, without the prior permission of the publishers.

Any person who commits any unauthorized act in relation to this publication may be liable to legal prosecution and civil claims for damages.

The age group that matches the content of the books has been classified according to the age classification system issued by the National Media Council.

ISBN – 9789948817369 – (Paperback)
ISBN – 9789948817376 – (E-Book)

Application Number: MC-10-01-9206108
Age Classification: E

Printer Name: iPrint Global Ltd
Printer Address: Witchford, England

First Published 2022
AUSTIN MACAULEY PUBLISHERS FZE
Sharjah Publishing City
P.O Box [519201]
Sharjah, UAE
www.austinmacauley.ae
+971 655 95 202

My deepest gratitude goes out to my partner Martin Barwise, for guiding me inward to my self-discovery and to my son, Austin, for teaching me how to listen to the sounds of my soul. Thanks to the support of my parents, Mariana and Joe Valentin and Will Fourie, I had the opportunity to follow my heart. And of course, I'd like to acknowledge my dear sister, Vicky-Ann Fourie. She deserves the highest praises for encouraging me to let my soul sing to the hearts of the ones who are ready to hear, and to always speak without a hint of fear. She also came up with the idea for the cover, thanks sister-friend. Lastly, I would like to extend a special thank you to Austin Macauley Publishers for helping me make my dream a reality. Without these people, this book would not exist.

Foreword

Mine, Yours, Ours is a trilogy of long poems written to inspire. Written to help you, the reader, embrace the courage to do some soul-searching. There are no requirements regarding the use of this book. There are, however, a few suggestions should you desire to indulge in the full experience of this book's intended purpose.

The purpose of this book is not only to serve as an artistic expression of the soul residing in me, as Marike Fourie. Its purpose is far more profound than its author. The purpose of this book is for *you* to find *your own* meaning in this creative experience.

What truly matters is that you realize that I did not create this piece of work to say anything specific to you. Truly, there is nothing I can say that would have an impact as deep and powerful as that of your own experience of *life*.

This is the reason why I created this poetic activity; so that you may, for yourself, discover experientially what you would call "Mine."

Introduction

Poetry is a timeless art form which has been reviving and redefining itself over the last few decades. It is an art form that is starting to grow exponentially as more and more people become aware of their creativity and understanding of *life*.

As I discovered my love for writing and passion for poetry, I noticed how most poets would create a collection of poems to be published in a single book. However, I had a slightly different vision for my poetry.

I remember first falling in love with poetry in high school. When we deciphered poems in our English Literary class, I always enjoyed making my own evaluations separately from the teacher's. I often preferred my own explanations of the poems, especially because it gave the poems meaning in my personal life.

Of course, I had to study the notes given by the teachers, but I always believed that poetry was meant for more than just understanding what the author might have meant with the metaphors, puns, and funky phrases.

I believe that poetry is like a painting made up of words and subliminal messages. It paints a picture, sparks a thought, and inspires a feeling within the observer; or in this case, the reader.

I believe the best way to honor the art of poetry is by deciphering the personal meaning it has to *you*, not by trying to understand exactly what the poet might have meant with each word, spacing, or punctuation mark.

The purpose of poetry, to me, is to stimulate the creative thinking ability of every person who encounters it. To awaken the soulful senses of the individual and tempt all people to look within themselves, to understand themselves at a deeper level through the words of another.

That is why I have added the following recommendations regarding the use of this book.

Recommendations

★ Always keep a pen/pencil handy when reading (any book for that matter)
★ Make use of the writing spaces between phrases as well as at the back of each page
★ If you feel comfortable, take a few deep breaths before starting with the activity
★ Say 'thank You' in advance for the gifts of reading, poetry, creativity, and self-discovery
★ Refrain from overthinking and keep a gentle focus on your breathing throughout the experience
★ Go slow, and fall into the flow of creativity
★ Look to what you feel with each verse, then try to articulate the words that best describe it
★ Relax and have fun

Mine

Mine

Was a dark and cold mine,

Was not a gold mine;

Was never even mine

To begin with.

But *mine*

Was always going to be a fine line,

Was always going to be an **endless** mine…

Will only always be *mine*

To be done with.

Mine

Was a short and tiny line,

Was not a shiny white line;

Was never only a line

To begin with.

But mine

Was always beautiful and fine,

Was always going to be an endless line…

Will only always be mine

To be done with.

It's mine!

My life.

My strife.

My knife.

My afterlife…

Not yet!

Because it's still mine

And no one else's.

Mine

I tried to hide.

I smiled so wide,

But was dead inside

Because of mind.

My mind

I tried to pride,

Instead, was snide.

I could not confide

In mine.

Mine

Had me a crave,

Turned me a slave;

Yet made me brave

Because of mine.

My mind

Was not a fave,

Rambled in a rave;

Almost made me cave…

I had to save

Mine!

It's mine!

My life.

My strife.

My knife.

My afterlife…

But not yet!

Because it's still *mine*

And no one else's.

Mine

Could not destroy,

Knew it was no toy;

Had more to deploy

through mine.

My mind

Was still coy,

Weary of joy;

Was only a decoy

For *mine*.

Mine

Was ready to heal,
Wanted more to feel!
Was done with the kneel
Of mind.

My mind
Mine made appeal,
Mine broke the seal;
Mine filled with zeal
My mind.

It's mine!

My hole.

My role.

My **soul**.

My goal…

To be whole yet!

Because it's only *mine*

And no one else's.

Mine

Was truly sublime.

Though it took some time;

Was worth the crime

Of mind.

My mind

Was not the "*I'm*,"

Nor the Prime.

Was only the climb

For mine.

Mine

Was starting to find

What's honest and kind;

Was never blind

Of mind.

My mind

Was not left behind,

Was becoming refined;

Was being **mined**

By *mine*.

It's *mine*!

My hole.

My role.

My soul.

My goal…

To be **whole** yet!

Because it's only mine

And no one else's.

Mine

Accepted the shame,

Acknowledged the blame;

Remembered the name

Of *mine*.

My mind

Was making tame

Its reference frame,

To Know The Game

Of *mine*.

Mine

Was not to attain,
Was not for the gain;
Was for the reign
Of *mine*.

My mind
Had to endure pain;
Had to go insane,
To remove all vain
From mine.

It's mine!

My story.

My quarry.

My allegory.

My glory…

Forever yet!

Because it's always *mine*

And no one else's.

Mine

Began as a school;

Taught by a fool

To become a tool

Of mind.

My mind

Thought mine was cruel,

Yet remembered the **jewel**;

Then grasped the rule

Of *mine*.

Mine

Knew what to do,

Brilliantly broke through;

Went back to the **hue**

Of *mine*.

My mind

Had no loose screw,

Had been made anew

And now stays true

To *mine*.

It's *mine*!

My story.

My quarry.

My allegory.

My **glory**…

Forever yet!

Because it's always mine

And no one else's.

Mine

Will never be done,
Will shine like the sun;
Will always be One
With mind.

My mind
Will never be won,
No longer holds a gun;
Will only be run
With mine.

Mine

Had been set free

Of the world's scree;

Has a loving spree

With mind.

My mind

Was filled with glee,

Had nothing to plea;

No longer wanted to flee

From mine.

It's mine!

My life; my strife.

My hole; my role.

My story; my glory.

My journey; yet…

It's always *mine*,

AND everyone else's!

Mine

Was, at last, aligned;
Could no longer be defined,
Was entirely entwined
With *mine*.

My mind
Had been willingly unwind,
And assuredly reassigned
To serve humankind
For *mine*.

Mine

Had to be shared,

To show that I cared;

I'm glad that I spared

Mine.

My mind

Will never again be scared

Now that *mine* had declared:

"**I am** eternally prepared,

And can never be compared

By mine."

It's *mine*!

My life; my strife.
My hole; my role.
My story; my glory.

My journey; yet…
It's always mine,
AND everyone else's!

Mine

Was a dark and cold wine,

Was not a gold wine;

Was never even mine

To be done with.

But mine

Was always going to be a fine wine,

Was always going to be a **timeless** wine…

Will only always be *mine*

To begin with.

Mine

Was a thin and twisted line,

Was not a straight and narrow line;

Was never only a line

To be done with.

But *mine*

Was always beautiful and fine,

Was always going to be an endless line…

Will only always be mine

To **begin** with.

Journaling space:

Yours

You know that no one can blame you,

You went with what life had you do.

The masses overshadowed the few,

Yet you never knew even this too.

You just wanted to fit into

The world's view

Of you.

But then you lost sight of Who

You came here to

Be – *You*!

Because somewhere **inside**, you knew

You wanted something new,

Something "the outside" couldn't offer you:

You wanted to know *you*.

It was a dark and cold night.
You were shivering with fright
After what some would call a delight;
You just realized your own might.
But the truth didn't seem to be right…

Because you looked at "the outside"
Despite all that you had to hide,
There was nothing you hadn't tried.
So, you chose to turn to your **inside**;
You just realized the world had lied!

But the story didn't only start then.

It already started way back when

All you knew were the words of men,

And you still lived in your mother's den.

Why did you choose to come back again?

You came down with burning questions,

Therefore, you had to be conditioned

To fit into "the outside's" positions.

Yet, you still had your premonitions,

Because *you* came here with your mission.

And so, it goes on as it had been going.

At first you had your inner *knowing*,

But then little baby kept growing.

Your intuition had to be slowing;

So, the information just kept on flowing.

"The outside" had mastered the teaching

Of killing your inside's reaching.

You **chose** to trust the world's preaching,

All your own rules they were breaching,

But you just kept on leeching.

This is yours

All of the chores,

Keeping scores;

Even more sores.

And nothing else,

But closed doors…

At least it's yours,

And no one else

can take it;

So, *you* take it.

You keep on keeping on

Because you choose to be strong,

Yet you cannot help but long

To know why it feels so wrong.

Why everything feels like a con…

You yearn for a place **to belong**,

Even from the day you were born.

That's why you wake up after dawn

Despite feeling like you are torn;

Inside, you knew that you were a pawn.

Oh, eat, sleep, work, repeat;
You've accepted "the outside's" defeat.
As long as your house looks neat
You have earned yourself a seat
On the Titanic's floundering fleet.

Because the damage was too discrete,
You didn't know that you had been beat.
You wished to be like the elite.
They shared with you a sickening treat
Until bullshit was all you could eat.

But once you noticed that you were falling

You stayed focused, you kept on crawling.

That's what you'll do to "one day" be balling.

Apparently, that's everyone's calling.

Your baggage was all you were hauling.

But at least you were making a killing

Even though it was not that fulfilling.

You thought that you had been willing

To do what "the outside" was drilling

Into you; till your baggage was spilling.

This is *yours*

All the chores,

Keeping scores;

Even more sores.

And nothing else,

But closed doors…

At least it's yours,

And no one else

can take it;

So, you take it.

Until you can't take it anymore…

"Okay, just wait a minute!
You don't have to be in it;
Since you clearly can't seem to win it."
That's how your mind may spin it,
But then why did you even begin it?

This is not how you wanted to spend it.
You didn't come just so you can lend it,
But now your **whole** inside is blended
And you don't know how to mend it.
You guess you might as well end it…

Oh, but what about your **purpose**?

There must be more to life than this!

Life wasn't meant to be lived lifeless;

Perhaps "the outside" can offer you bliss.

Maybe you turned to a stranger's kiss.

Any escape that comes with ease,

Anything that can instantly please,

Make you forget about your disease;

Turn to pills and bottles and tease

Till *your inner world* was ceased.

This is no author's opinion;
This is merely an observation
Of the general incarnation
Or your current condemnation
Of humanity's nation of separation.

But your focus is on the recession;
By now, all you know is retention.
No wonder you're filled with depression;
It's an effect of "mass oppression,"
But it'll **change** once you set the *intention*.

This is yours.

But, of course
It came with force.
Now, filled with remorse
And nothing else;
Yours is off-course.

At least it's yours,
And no one else
can take it;
So, *you* take it.

But it can't keep on like it's been;
The **truth** had already been seen.
Only few know what it means.
And suddenly, you are keen
To make sense of *everything*.

Alas, you start with the healing.
It hurts, when it's all that you're feeling,
But at least you started dealing
With your inner pain that was squealing,
And the "lies" that had you kneeling.

Hoorah! What a beautiful process!

You **awaken** and choose to protest,

To bring awareness to all you're against.

You believe you no longer digress,

You believe you can pass the test.

Though you still think this place is a mess.

Your biggest battle is still stress.

You change the way that you dress

And keep reaching for your crest;

But now you see **the outside** as 'less.'

You're clearly still figuring it out,
What this reality is all about.
Your current mission is simply to scout
'Cause you still seem to have some doubt;
Your *awareness* has started to sprout.

You've stopped fearing being **alone**,
You no longer choose to moan;
You've discovered a ***higher*** tone.
Your mind was bashed and blown;
You saw how life's fabric was sown.

This is *yours*.

But, of course

It came with force,

Caused some remorse

And nothing else;

Yours was off-course.

At least it's yours,

And no one else

can take it;

So, you take it.

Until you can't take it anymore…

Oh, the wonder of being awaken;
Of realizing you'd been mistaken
For holding on to what had been taken.
Your whole world had to be shaken
To *grasp* what it's really been making.

This time "the outside" won't win,
Since you let its full weight sink in.
You understood where it had to begin,
You're finally comfortable inside your skin
'Cause you've accepted **everything**.

You have fallen into the flow

And detached your own ego,

Because **now** you truly know

How deep *your* soul can go.

As above, **so it shall be below**.

Now, all you desire is to grow,

So that you may be able to show

To the ones who still do not know;

They don't have to stay on their toes,

Unless that was what they chose.

But for you, there is no more battle.

No longer 'the sleeping' are cattle,

No longer you choose to tattle

Or indulge in preconceived prattle.

You prefer not to cause a rattle.

Aah, your inside is unwound.

Your deepest truth had been found

Though you had to be knocked to the ground,

So that you may have heard the sound

Of the *love* that is all around.

This is yours.

All the edgy shores

That required restores

Which led you to *your source*.

And nothing else,

But **all that is**,

Yours.

At last, it's *yours*!

And no one else

can take it;

So, you take it

Until you can't keep it anymore.

Finally, you're awake in your play!
There is so much you have to say;
All this truth that has come your way
Could perhaps brighten someone's day.
You yearn to give it all away.

Though you're conscious of how they behave,
You now see that your people are brave.
Yet their **freedom** is something you crave,
So you may deliver them from the grave;
But there still is nothing to save…

Because there is no more wrong or right,
You rejoice in your brothers' delight,
Extend help when they're filled with fright
And bring new ideas into their sight;
But you do this without a fight.

Since you have nothing more to hide,
No longer are you chasing your Pride
Because you know Who you are *inside*.
You flow freely with life's tide,
And at last, you're enjoying the ride.

Now you'll always be an example.
You know that you alone are ample,
You know your outside is a **temple**,
You will never again choose to trample;
You are part of the new human sample.

You are a light for others to follow,
For those souls who may still feel hollow,
Who were stuck for too long in the wallow
Of the unconscious and the shallow;
So *their* **inside** again they may know.

This is *yours*.

All the edgy shores

That required restores

Which led you to your **source**.

And nothing else,

But All That Is,

Yours.

At last, it's yours!

And no one else

can take it;

So, you take it

And you give it *forevermore*…

Now you know that <u>nothing can hurt you</u>,

So, you go with, wherever life leads you;

Your worries and fears became few.

Yet, you never knew even this, too;

You *already* fit **perfectly** into

The Grandest view

Of you!

Then you gained sight of who

You came here to

Be – **You**.

Because somewhere inside, you knew

You wanted something new,

Something "the outside" couldn't offer you:

You wanted to know *you*.

Journaling space:

Ours

It took hours upon hours,
But now we're here.

It took showers upon showers,
But now we're near.

It took scours upon scours,
But now we're clear.

It took flowers upon flowers,
But now we endear…

'Cause it's ours, it's ours
Everything we fear.

Ours

Is a mess!

Picking flowers,

We digressed;

Picking trees,

Mother's stressed.

But we continue to undress,

To replace our nest

With towers

That claim they are the best…

Because all we want is

Ours.

It's time to address an issue,

To have a real discussion;

One that's long overdue.

It's not just a superstition,

The sky had become less blue.

The ground is in need of remission,

Even the clouds are less colorful too.

Because of destructive repetition

We changed the atmosphere's hue;

It's all part of the king's fruition.

So, let us start talking
About the demolition
That has kept us sinking;

About the cause of our inhibition,
The orders given by the king
That caused all this disruption.
What the hell was he thinking?

Crowned by greed and ambition;
Head up, his puppets kept walking.
They lived only for their mission.

There is so much that is hidden.

That's why the walls had been built,

To disguise the truth that is written.

Yet, the king still knew no guilt.

For his entire life he had only ridden

Trojan horses saddled with a quilt.

Only self-gain ever had him smitten.

As our people started to wilt,

The king chew even *more* than he had bitten

And we lived off the crumbs that he spilt.

Ours

Is a mess!

Picking flowers,

We digressed;

Picking trees,

Mother's stressed.

But we continue to undress,

To replace our nest

With towers

That claim they are the best…

Because all we want is

Ours.

We idolized our own oppressor.

We called the king our friend.

Hanging on the words of the professor

When education was a means to an end.

Thus, they only taught the lesser,

To make the majority bend

To the will of the king and his successor.

Because royalty never knew how to fend.

They never learnt how to handle the pressure.

All they really knew was how to spend.

This was the world that we made;

At least at some point in time.

'Cause the structure had started to fade.

At least, now we can make a dime.

At least, now we get paid

Enough to afford a lemon or lime;

Enough for survival and shade.

Yet, we did not see the clear crime,

The king's colossal crusade;

The Prime of the **old paradigm**.

For too long this was the case:

Blindly living with our backs bent over,

Just to be part of the race.

We cared not for the exposure,

We cared only to increase our pace;

To collect every four-leaf clover.

But we can't avoid leaving a trace.

Will we ever find closure?

Will the truth be what we embrace?

Or will we keep wandering like the outcast rover?

Ours

Is a test.

Picking flowers,

Like human pest!

Picking ease;

We put to rest.

The lies that must still be confessed,

Because it's too great a quest.

For hours

We'll chase our crest,

Because all we care about is

Ours.

But is there really someone to blame

For the way in which we're living?

Who first changed the rules of the game?

This can perhaps be unnerving,

But *things never stay the same.*

Though we are definitely deserving

Of the queen's infamous fame.

But instead, we are still serving

The system that had made us tame.

While our hearts are dead, **starving**.

We forgot that it's all up to us,
That *we* can make things right.
Instead, we just made a big fuss;

Instead, we just made a big fight.
We blamed each other, we scream and cuss.
And, much to the queen's delight
We had chosen not to discuss

That which was not in plain sight.
We rather threw it under the bus.
We only had *each other* to spite.

So, we kept listening to the mainstream,

To the facts most easily attained.

We accept things the way that they seem.

More hatred was all that we gained.

We continued to cuss and scream

At our brothers who were also chained,

And our sisters who did not deem

Themselves **worthy**, for they were too pained.

Not knowing how to become a team.

Therefore, chaos was all that remained.

Ours

Is a test.

Picking flowers,

Like human pest!

Picking ease,

We put to rest.

The lies that must still be confessed

Because it's too great a quest.

For hours

We'll chase our crest.

Because all we care about is

Ours.

It had been years since the king had died.

The queen ate him; now she is *immortal*.

So she may keep his principles applied

That civilization lived only by his morals.

She carried her new crown with Pride

And made sure her castle had no portals,

Because no commoner may come **inside**.

Though her behavior was blatantly immoral,

It went unseen; we let the massacre slide.

Until somehow, the truth became oral…

Just when all hope seemed to be lost

Some angels chose to incarnate.

Apparently, there's a line we had crossed.

Thus, news reached Heaven's gate.

All compassion on Earth had been tossed,

We had allowed our egos to inflate.

Our hearts had become numb with frost.

Fortunately, *it's never too late*.

History is still worth all it had cost.

We can still make the future great.

But for that, many things had to change.

Society needed to **evolve**;

We needed to increase our frequency range.

<u>No problem is ever too big to solve</u>;

The angels had plans to arrange.

Nothing is ever too bad to involve

God Almighty; we will not derange.

That's *where* we reside till we decide to devolve,

To become human; an experience so strange,

When there is something we want to resolve.

Ours

Is a *quest*.

Picking flowers,

We made ourselves less;

Picking bees,

Mother started to press.

To remind us how much we are **blessed**.

That on Earth, we are simply a guest

And vast powers

Are what we possess.

Because all we can control is

Ours.

So, we chose to turn to the truth once more.
We realized that we can't blame each other,
Nor can we blame the queen's war.

Because fault will always find another.
Criticism is always uncalled for.
When we take responsibility for our brothers,
The human family will again start to **soar**.

When we start to listen to our dear Mother,
When we *remember* what it means to adore;
Then all the sadness can be smothered.

It will not be an easy task;

Of this we can be assured.

There's a question we first need to ask:

Do we believe that we can be cured?

There are a few things we need to unmask;

Our attitudes must become matured.

We must empty our toxic flask.

Only then can we become secured.

Yet, we will only truly bask

Once we *heal* what the world had endured.

Yes, we have to forgive the queen.

We must first find inner peace,

And let go of all the 'bad' we've seen.

'Cause even royalty slips on grease;

Even the devil's slate is wiped clean.

Even *love* will only increase

Once the **lover** decides to be keen.

And as we start to pick up each piece

The outcome becomes foreseen;

We *will* iron out every little crease!

Ours

Is a quest.

Picking flowers,

We made ourselves less;

Picking bees,

Mother started to press.

To remind us how much we are blessed.

That on Earth, we are simply a guest

And vast powers

Are what we possess.

Because all we can control is

Ours.

Now, the time has finally come

For this human reality to improve.

It's time to throw away the war drum.

For separation to be what we remove.

Even the best quality is **equal** to scum.

Now, we must change our groove;

To take care of our siblings and Mum.

Away from fear we shall move

Until every person becomes our chum,

Because *there is nothing left to prove.*

There are some facts we cannot deny;

Our **home** is in need of great care.

But instead of pondering why

Let us rather choose to share
Accountability for every little lie
That may have caused us to tear
Apart the Earth and the sky.

'Cause the truth is we do have a flair
To show a *love* of the ***highest*** high;
A human quality that used to be rare.

We cannot disprove our *connection*;

Our hearts know we are inseparable

Despite our physical complexion.

Together our strength is immeasurable;

Alone, we only know objection.

Let all of us become vulnerable,

Let us be overwhelmed with affection.

So we may know that we are venerable,

Then *together* we will cure Mother's infection

And choose to do only what is honorable.

Ours

Is a game like chess…

Picking flowers,

We no longer obsess;

Picking keys,

We've unlocked our treasure chest.

We're worth more than we ever could've guessed.

Now, we go forward with zest;

And Mother showers

Us with whatever we request.

Because all we have is

All we give,

And **everything** is still

Ours.

It took hours upon hours,
But now we're here.

It took showers upon showers,
But now we're near.

It took scours upon scours,
But now we're clear.

It took flowers upon flowers,
But now we endear…

'Cause it's ours, it's ours
Everything we find here!

Journaling space: